Let's Go to Build a Skyscraper

Everyone likes to be a sidewalk superintendent—to peer through a hole in the fence to watch a building going up. Now you can peek through that hole to learn about everything from the complicated planning of the modern skyscraper, through the twenty-two months it takes from the digging of the foundation, until the moment the building is ready for people to move into the apartments, offices, and stores.

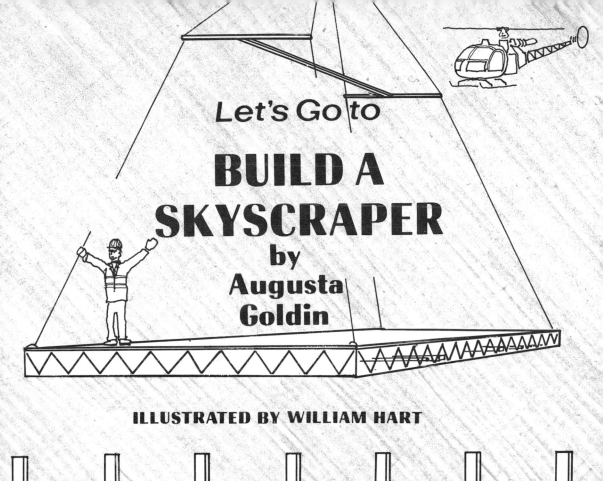

Let's Go to
BUILD A
SKYSCRAPER
by
Augusta
Goldin

ILLUSTRATED BY WILLIAM HART

G. P. PUTNAM'S SONS, NEW YORK

Acknowledgments

For technical assistance in the writing of this book, the author is indebted to the Tishman Realty and Construction Company, particularly John L. Tishman, executive vice-president in charge of construction, and Bert Weinstein, project manager, Tower A of the World Trade Center.

The author also wishes to thank Leonard Reider, Catskill Mountains construction expert; Bill Fain, architect of Midtown Planning and Development, the Mayor's Office, New York City; and Angelo Amatulli, Chairman, Department of Structural Technology, Brooklyn Technical High School.

Here comes the future!

And here comes a super modern skyscraper! This is a mixed-use high-riser. It's designed for people to work in, shop in, play in, and live in.

It's going up right now, on the drawing boards. Spanning half a dozen railroad tracks. Reaching down into the bedrock. Rising up to the sky.

Let's go see the site. There it is, a six-acre railroad yard, steel-ribbed and bare. Five years from now, this site will look like a city in the sky. It will glitter with towering buildings. It will be trimmed with stainless steel and ribboned with blue-green glass. It will be filled with people—hustling and bustling.

SITE BEFORE CONSTRUCTION

Look at the rendering of the first eighty-story tower. It rises like a shaft from the wide plaza.

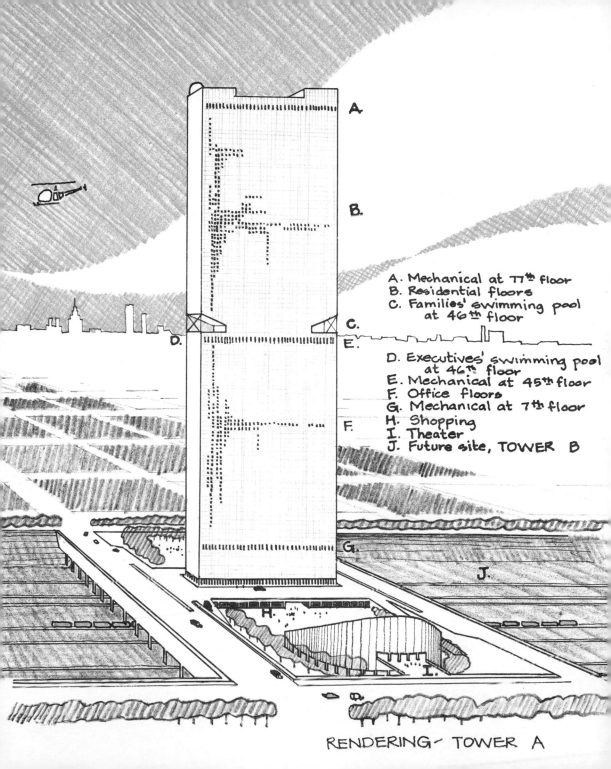

A. Mechanical at 77th floor
B. Residential floors
C. Families' swimming pool
   at 46th floor

D. Executives' swimming pool
   at 46th floor
E. Mechanical at 45th floor
F. Office floors
G. Mechanical at 7th floor
H. Shopping
I. Theater
J. Future site, TOWER B

RENDERING - TOWER A

There's the main lobby at street level. Below that is the mall with specialty shops, bookstores, restaurants, and a supermarket. Above the lobby are seventy-eight additional stories. Forty-one are for offices, and three for mechanical floors. From these three floors, mechanical systems will service the building. Here the water-pumping systems will be located. Here the heating, cooling, ventilating, and air-scrubbing machines will operate. Here the pneumatic systems for deliveries and garbage disposal will respond to computer control.

And up under the roof garden are thirty-two stories for apartments, studios, a medical center, a gym, and a kindergarten school.

The top two floors are special. The seventy-ninth features a children's library, a playground, a garden, and a restaurant. The

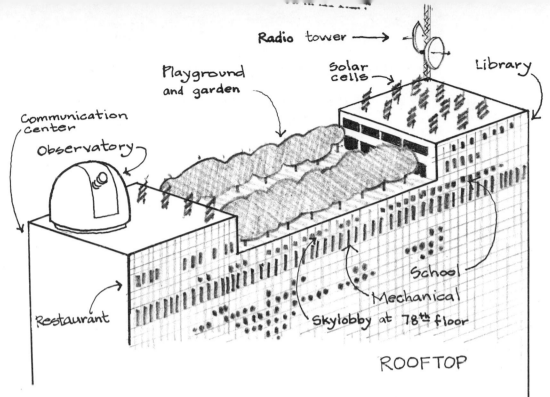

Radio tower →

Playground and garden

Solar cells →

Library

Communication center

Observatory

Restaurant

School

Mechanical

Skylobby at 78th floor

ROOFTOP

eightieth is reserved for a twenty-first-century communication and power center. Here, on a platform near the rooftop garden, is the observatory. And there, on another platform is the radio tower next to the solar cells which will heat and cool the tower.

Look again at the rendering. You will see skylobbies, playgrounds, and two swimming pools, one for families. Each pool is both an indoor and outdoor pool.

they're enclosed by fitted screens. On bright and sunny days the screens fold back automatically.

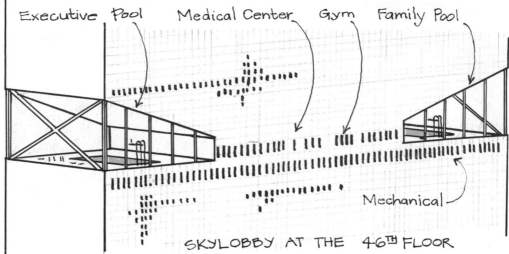

Executive Pool   Medical Center   Gym   Family Pool

Mechanical

SKYLOBBY AT THE 46TH FLOOR

Both pools are located on the forty-sixth floor. Why not the eightieth? The architects advised against that. They explained that tall buildings always sway a little when the wind blows up a storm. In a roaring hurricane this skyscraper would sway quite a few inches. Such a sway would make waves in a rooftop pool. Then the water would slosh over and out!

This tower will be beautiful and exciting, but no one will be moving into it for at least three years. That's because hundreds of plans have to be made. And all of them have to be checked out by the city building department before construction crews are allowed onto the site.

So the Twenty-First-Century Development Company begins planning. It completes the purchase of the property. It buys the air rights for the airspace over the railroad

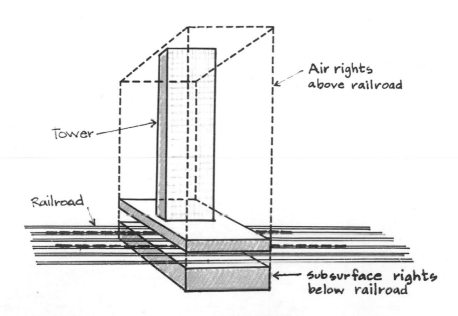

PURCHASE RIGHTS DIAGRAM

tracks. Here it will erect the skyscraper. And it buys the rights for the land *under* the railroad tracks. Here it will construct three sub-basement garages.

Then the company calls in the experts. It hires a firm of building consultants made up of architects and engineers.

Right away, the surveyors move their transits and other instruments onto the site. Theirs is a double assignment:

1. They have to survey and map the area and locate the utility lines. These may be on

the surface or buried under the tracks.

2. They have to make test borings down to the bedrock. Then they'll know how far down the footings have to be sunk.

Footings support the weight of the building. They are made of concrete and steel rods and look like this:

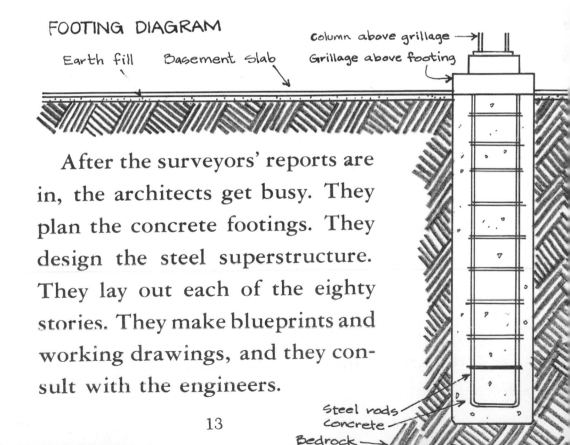

FOOTING DIAGRAM

Earth fill   Basement Slab

Column above grillage →
Grillage above footing

After the surveyors' reports are in, the architects get busy. They plan the concrete footings. They design the steel superstructure. They lay out each of the eighty stories. They make blueprints and working drawings, and they consult with the engineers.

Steel rods
Concrete
Bedrock →

The structural engineers work out the details for construction. And they write up the specifications. This means they specify the exact kinds, sizes, amounts, and qualities of the thousands of items that will be needed.

At the same time, mechanical and electrical engineers plan the utility systems to be installed on the mechanical floors. And they, too, write up their specifications.

One more team of specialists swings in, the interior space planners. They are the experts on wall facings, floor coverings, light fixtures, and room dividers. And their specifications read like this:

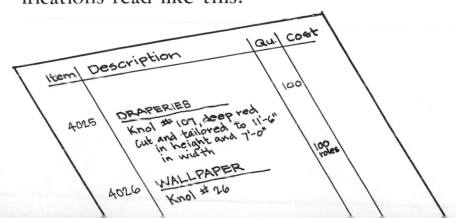

Item	Description	Qu.	Cost
		100	
4025	DRAPERIES Knol # 107, deep red cut and tailored to 11'-6" in height and 7'-0" in width		
4026	WALLPAPER Knol # 26	100 roles	

After nine months the plans are completed. The building will definitely be a landmark, but it will cost a fortune.

Naturally the company is interested in keeping the costs down. So it advertises for bidding in the major building journals.

The Twenty-First-Century Development Company Invites Bids for the construction of Tower A, a first of a complex.
- **Write for information concerning instructions and specifications**
- **Sealed bids will be received and publicly opened on June 9, at 11 A.M.**

Address the Twenty-First-Century Development Company
        . . . N.Y.C. Offices.

Bids begin arriving in the mail. On the advertised date, all the envelopes are opened publicly. One construction company bids

$1,500,000 a floor. Others bid from $1,700,000 to $2,000,000 a floor.

The owners of the Twenty-First-Century Development Company consider the bids carefully. They accept the most favorable one and announce the name of the winning construction company. From now on, that company's construction superintendent will be in charge of the project.

But the project cannot get started yet because the owners must first get permission to build. They must apply to the city building department for an assortment of working permits.

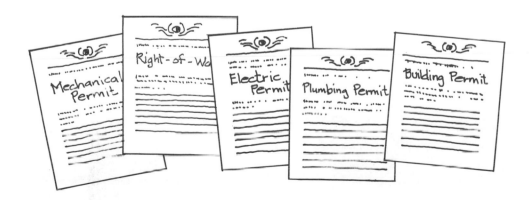

The city wants to be sure that this tower will satisfy the building codes and the zoning laws. Some cities do not allow skyscrapers to block air and light from other buildings and streets.

Although hundreds of people have been working on the project for more than a year, it is all paper work. But as soon as the permits are granted, construction may begin.

Now the bulldozers start rumbling down the street. They clatter onto the site, between the railroad tracks, and up, onto the higher right-of-way. The mobile cranes and

dump trucks chug right behind. They smoke, and sputter, and snort.

The bulldozers crash through. They clear the area and level it.

The cranes swivel. They hoist. They dump the debris onto the trucks.

The trucks haul it away, roaring and bumping over the railroad tracks. And ten

minutes later that debris is dumped on the lower embankment and becomes landfill.

In a few days the site is ready for groundbreaking. This means the workers will then begin constructing the garages beneath the tracks.

Now the construction superintendent moves his office onto a corner of the property. His office is a mammoth trailer, equipped with thousands of blueprints that

T.V. CONTROL

← COMPUTER

MAP RACK #1

are bound in files and hung from racks. A closed-circuit television hookup will let him see what's going on in any part of the project. A two-way radio system will let him talk to the foremen on the job. And a computer, set into the wall, will develop a timetable. Then it will let him know if the work is going according to schedule. Every week the computer will issue reports called printouts. These will show which crews' work is

on time and which crews are lagging behind. They will pinpoint trouble spots. And they will indicate other ways of working out these trouble spots.

On the morning of groundbreaking day, the hard hats report to the site with their huge machines: the backhoes and jackhammers, the cement mixers, pumps, vibrators, and heavy cranes. They are going to use twenty-first-century building methods and build the underground retaining walls before they excavate the basement!

Some rip up the streets according to plan.

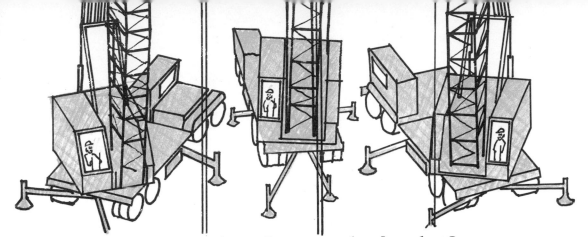

Some dig trenches down to bedrock. Some pipe slurry into the trenches. (Slurry is a thick mixture of clay and water that keeps the sides of the trench from caving in.)

Other workers lower preassembled steel cages into the slurry.

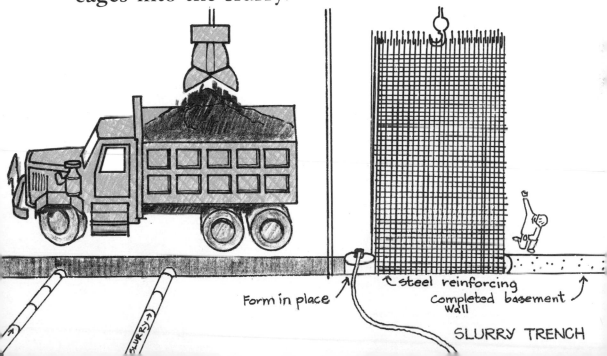

Form in place

steel reinforcing

Completed basement wall

SLURRY TRENCH

Then the slurry is piped out, concrete is piped in, the whole thing hardens, and the concrete retaining walls, reinforced by the steel cages, are done. They're also invisible, but not for long. Because now the three sub-basement garages are going to be excavated.

Riding high, the excavation crew rolls in. Cranes and dump trucks, backhoes, multihoes, and power shovels crowd the area. Dust flies. Motors whine and screech. The racket is deafening. And a crew stands by with woven steel mats to contain the flying debris.

The digging continues. The basement hole gets bigger and bigger. Bracing studs, girders, and columns get longer and heavier. And the city's building inspector keeps checking for safety.

When the hole is three stories deep and the retaining walls have been uncovered, the

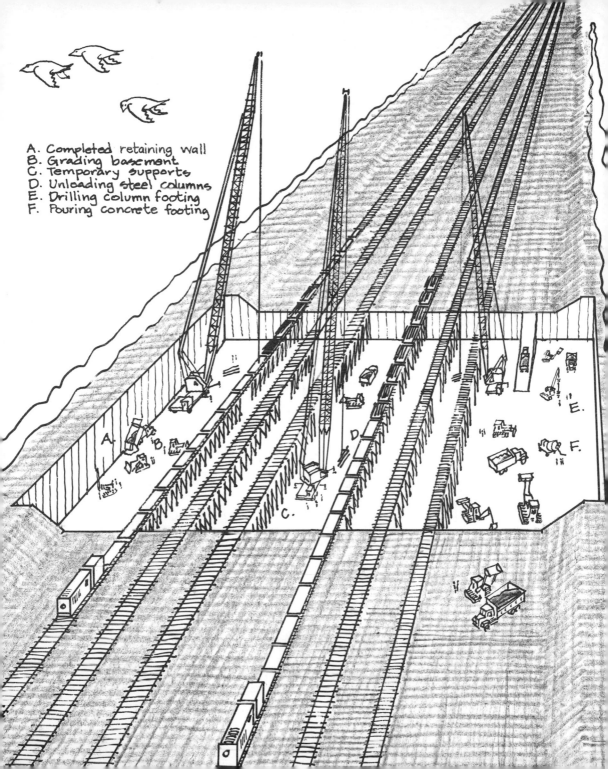

A. Completed retaining wall
B. Grading basement
C. Temporary supports
D. Unloading steel columns
E. Drilling column footing
F. Pouring concrete footing

excavation stops. Now the footings have to be made.

According to plan, the footings are to be sunk below the railroad tracks. So holes are drilled down into the bedrock. Then bars are carefully positioned into the holes. After that, the holes are filled with concrete.

As soon as all the footings are in place, each one is topped with a two-ton grillage. A grillage is a framework of steel beams, strong enough to support the tall steel for the tower. It's lifted and put into place by the cranes. It's lined up by the steelworkers so it's absolutely plumb, meaning vertical, and absolutely level, meaning horizontal.

GRILLAGE A3

Then the work crews return to the sub-basements. The floors and ceilings are framed out. Concrete is piped in and smoothed down, and the garages, way down under the tracks, are finished.

Finally, fifteen months after the planning started, the steel columns begin to rise from the grillages.

Work on the core of the tower starts first. This is to be the service and elevator area. In the core, local and express elevators will carry men and materials to their work stations. The core will also stiffen the building. That's because it's tied down to the foundation. The core will serve as a base for the giant cranes which lift the air-conditioning units, the pumps, and the heavy sections of floors and walls, all made of structural steel.

For building skyscrapers, there's nothing as strong as structural steel. And it is made still stronger by being manufactured in the shape of the letter I or H. You can prove that this is so, by turning to the back of this book and doing the experiment that's described there. For this reason, I beams and H columns are most often used in building skyscrapers.

The core and outside walls of the tower continue to climb upward above the railroad tracks. These walls, like the core, stiffen the building and hold it rigid.

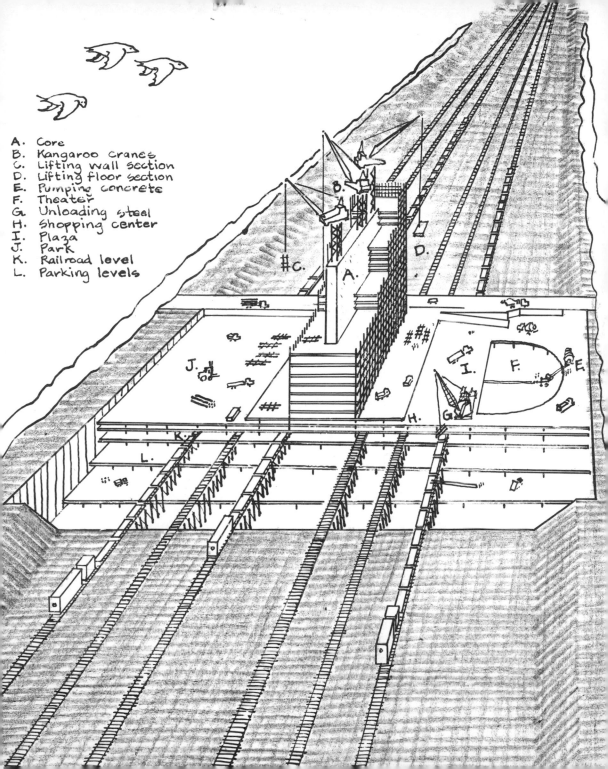

A. Core
B. Kangaroo cranes
C. Lifting wall section
D. Lifting floor section
E. Pumping concrete
F. Theater
G. Unloading steel
H. Shopping center
I. Plaza
J. Park
K. Railroad level
L. Parking levels

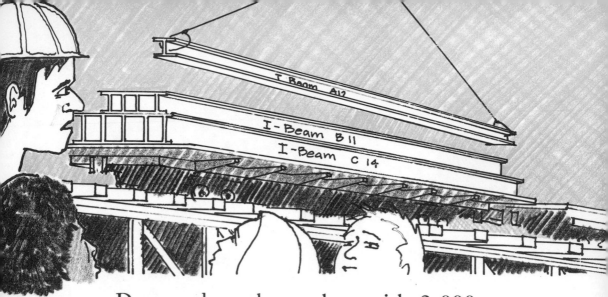

Days and weeks go by, with 2,000 men on the job. The computer reports that work is moving according to schedule. That's because deliveries are moving according to schedule. And this is made possible at the steel mills. There each of the beams and prebuilt panels is numbered for placement in certain parts of the tower. Then the computer calls for these numbered items. It calls for them to be delivered on the day and on the hour that they're needed on the job. Then flatbed trains cart them to the site, loaded according to specification.

Another thing that keeps the schedule moving is the use of twenty-first-century wall and floor systems.

The exterior walls are not built on the job. They're delivered in sections, three stories high and twelve feet wide. Each structural steel section weighs twenty-two tons, but it is swung into position easily by the giant cranes that straddle the core.

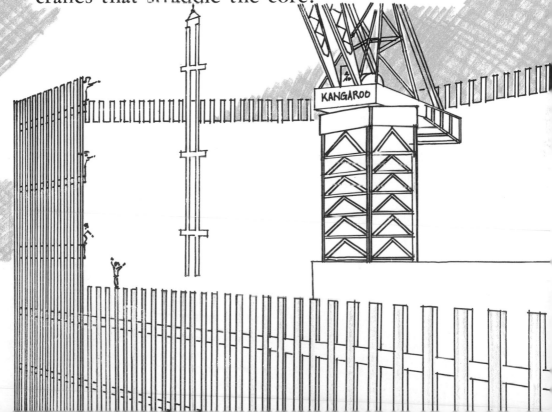

KANGAROO

The hard hats swarm all over the mighty beams. Using two-way radio communication, the raising gang gets the sections to the right story. The fitting-up gang fits them together with driftpins. The bolting-up gang bolts them together with pneumatic wrenches.

This is dangerous work. Imagine leaning into the wind on the seventy-fifth floor and trying to keep your balance on a horizontal beam or trying to duck a swinging wall section. Flexible rubber-soled shoes help. Special protective gloves help. But for falling objects, hard hats help the most.

I - Beam   R 14

Although hard hats are made only of plastic, they can take very hard knocks. That's because they are built on the principle of the arch. A falling brick, a wrench, or a hammer just bounces off them. These hats are so strong men could stand on them and nothing would happen.

In this skyscraper the floor systems move right along with the rising walls. According to specification, the floor units come in lengths that reach from core to exterior wall. They are very long units and very strong and thirty inches thick. Inside this thickness are the utility ducts. Inside, too, are the open-web steel beams that look like trusses. These

are so strong they will prevent the floors from collapsing.

Perched on portable scaffolds, scores of workers install these floor systems from underneath. Topside, others pour concrete into the decks.

Floors, walls, and core continue to rise. And three stories behind, the fireproofing crew follows. This crew sprays every inch of steel with a mixture of concrete and mineral fibers. Although steel is very strong, it can't stand intense heat. In a roaring fire, steel won't burn. It will soften and sag. Then the whole building might collapse. But when

steel is sprayed with this fireproofing mixture, it stays cool and solid.

Work proceeds as planned and on schedule. The building grows taller and taller. The men are now working on the seventy-sixth floor. On the eightieth.

TOPPING OFF

They've reached the top, and it's time for the topping off. The topping off is a magnificent party on the top of the building, which is topped with a magnificent evergreen tree. It is given by the owners for the 2,000 workers, the architects, engineers, space planners, inspectors, and important city officials. Bands play. Flags snap in the breeze. And as the last beam is lifted into place,

cranes bring up the refreshments: sand-
wiches, salad, fruit and cake, and cold drinks.
Everybody celebrates at topping off.

But the tower is still far from finished.

Far below, workers are busy covering the
exterior walls with thin stainless-steel panels.
And glaziers, operating huge suction-cup
machines, are easing quarter-inch plate glass
into place. These windows are made to with-
stand extra-strong wind. Since they are blue-
green, they reduce the heat and glare of the
sun.

When the last window has been set, the exterior of the skyscraper is finished. It is trimmed with stainless steel and ribboned with blue-green glass.

Now the plaza surrounding the building is overlaid with marble. The fountains are hooked up and tested. And the plaza is completed.

After that, a trailer painted with the house colors of the Twenty-First-Century Development Company pulls up and parks. This is the renting office. Here the renting agent

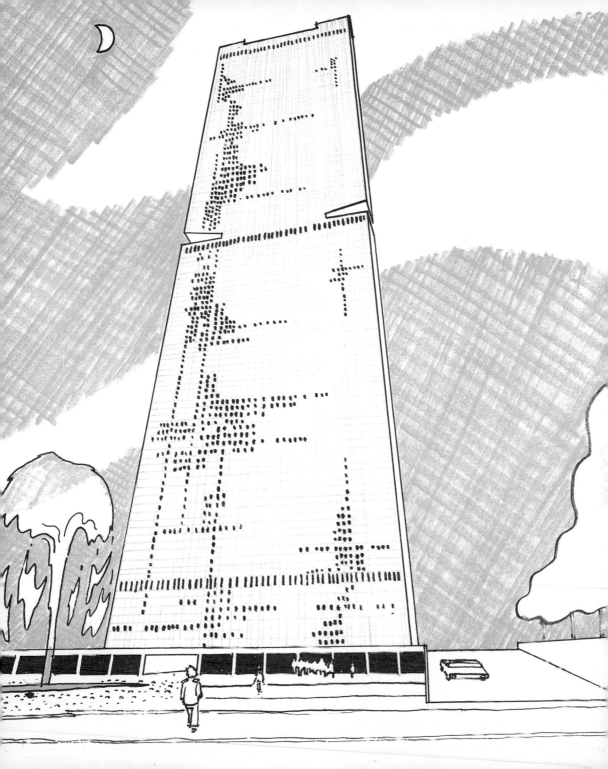

will explain floor plans, leases, and rents for the stores, offices, and apartments.

Still, no tenants can move in. That's because the inside is not ready. Inside, plumbers, plasterers, and painters hurry to finish. Telephone linemen monitor hookups. Space planners supervise the laying of carpet and the hanging of draperies. Plumbers and electricians make sure the mechanical systems are all right.

Outside, the tower is beautiful. But inside, it is still a mess. Stores, offices, apartments, and halls are littered with scraps of wood and wire, wallpaper and carpeting. Forgotten wheelbarrows, ladders, brackets, and nails are all over the floors.

So the pickup gang moves in to pick up the leftovers.

CLEAN-UP

And hard on their heels comes the clean-up gang. Vacuum cleaners hum. Mops and brushes fly. Rags soaked with wax and polish whisk over surfaces. Windows, woodwork, light fixtures, and tile begin to shine and gleam.

Now the building inspector stops in for a last safety check. If he finds any violations, the construction superintendent will have them corrected right away.

INSPECTION

Then a certificate of occupancy is issued. The tenants may now move in.

But it's not so easy to move in. The street is crowded with dump trucks, diesel engines, trailers, and cranes pulling out. Huge furni-

ture vans are trying to pull in. And the tenants start coming. Executives, couples, and families with children and pets arrive in their private cars. They admire the tall, glittering walls of Tower A. They drive down to the subbasement garages. They park beneath the railroad tracks. After that, they ride the elevators to their fine new quarters.

But everyone wants to see everything and explore everything first. So off they go to the specialty shops, the sky lobbies, the sky playgrounds, and the swimming pools with the folding screens. Then they go to the restaurant on the seventy-ninth floor. After lunch, they walk up to the eightieth floor to see the communications and power center and the view.

And what do they see eighty stories below? They see:

. . . Cranes being assembled by the hard hats near the tracks.

. . . Flatbed trains, laden with numbered steel beams, pulling up to the unloading area.

. . . And they see the construction

superintendent's office trailer being towed by a tractor to another corner of the property.

Tower B, another modern skyscraper, is going up!

Something to Do While Reading
Let's go to Build a Skyscraper

QUESTION: Why do engineers write specifications for steel that's shaped in the form of I beams or H columns?

ANSWER: Because the flanges and webs make the beams stronger. You can prove this by doing the following experiment.

Get a tube of airplane glue and 6 strips of balsa wood, 1/16 inch thick, 1/2 inch wide, and 12 inches long available at any store that sells model airplane kits. (Actually, you need only 3 strips, but get 6 just in case you break some.)

Pick up one of the strips and hold it horizontally. Use both hands, one at each end of the strip. Can you bend it? Of course! So, put 2 strips together, face to face. They will also bend easily.

Now re-position these 3 strips. This means you will fasten them together in different positions, in 3 steps:

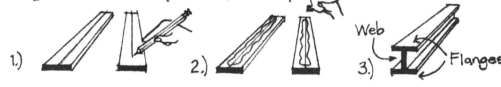

- In step 1, place 2 of the strips on your desk, and draw a middle line from end to end, on each.
- In step 2, spread glue over the pencilled lines.
- In step 3, paste the 3 strips together, to make an I beam.

Give the glue an hour to harden, then test your model for strength. Place 2 big books about 9 inches apart, on your desk. Span the space between the books with your I Beam. On it, balance a book or 2. Your beam will remain rigid. It will not bend. If you upend your model and hold it vertically (like an H column), it will also remain rigid when you put a weight on the top end!

Your conclusion? That simple strips bend easily; but when they are shaped with flanges and a web, they are much stronger. That's why engineers specify I beams and H columns!

Glossary

Architect—a person who designs buildings. (p. 12)

Air rights—permission to use the airspace over property that belongs to another person or another company. (p. 11)

Backhoe—a tractor with a rear hydraulic arm, to which is attached a toothed bucket that is used for digging. A multihoe is a backhoe with a front-end bucket that scoops up the excavated debris. (pp. 22 and 24)

Bedrock—the solid, unbroken rock which is part of the earth's crust. (p. 13)

Boring—a cylindrical hole that's dug straight down to the bedrock. (p. 13)

Certificate of Occupancy—a document issued by the city building department, which states that the building is safely constructed and may now be occupied. (p. 42)

Concrete—a mixture of cement, sand, gravel, and water, that hardens as it dries. For extra strength, concrete may be poured over a network of steel bars. (p. 24)

Core—the central part of the building. The core extends from the basement to the roof. It stiffens the building and houses the elevator shafts. (p. 27)

Debris—rubbish consisting of stones and boulders and/or other excavated material. (p. 20)

Flanges—the two outer parts of an I beam. (p. 45)

Footing—the part of the foundation that bears directly down on the earth (and, when possible, into the bedrock). (p. 13)

Grillage—a heavy framework of crossing beams that is used to support tall columns. (p. 26)

Hard hat—a protective helmet usually made of plastic or aluminum. Sometimes, the man who wears one is himself called a hard hat. (p. 22)

Level—generally called a spirit level. An instrument used to check horizontal positions. (p. 26)

Mechanical floors—special stories in a skyscraper, completely reserved for heating, air-conditioning, and electrical systems. (p. 8)

Plumb—a construction worker's term meaning vertical, or straight up and down. (p. 26)

Print-out—pages of information which are automatically printed out by the computer. (p. 21)

Rendering—a representation of a building to show how it will look when it is completed. (p. 6)

Retaining wall—a wall that's built to hold back the earth around an excavated area. (p. 22)

Scaffold—a raised platform on which carpenters and painters and other construction men work. (p. 34)

Site—the location where the building is to be erected. (p. 6)

Slurry—a thick, soupy mixture of clay and water. Slurry is piped into trenches, then allowed to harden and form retaining walls. (p. 23)

Specifications—detailed written descriptions of the particular items that are to be ordered so the skyscraper can be built. If, for example, doorknobs are to be ordered, the specifications will show: the number of doorknobs needed, the kinds required, the sizes, quality, and cost. (p. 14)

Surveyor—a person who determines scientifically the exact forms, boundaries, and position of a tract of land. (p. 12)

Tempered plate glass—flat sheets of glass that have been treated with heat to make them strong. (p. 37)

Topping off—a ceremony held on top of the building after the highest steel beam is lifted into place. (p. 36)

Transit—an instrument with a telescope attachment. It is used by surveyors for measuring angles. (p. 12)

Truss—a rigid framework of interlocking triangles. (p. 34)

Utilities—the public services (gas, water, electricity, and telephone) that are built in when the building is erected. (p. 14)

Utility lines—wires, mains, cables, and pipes that carry the gas, water, electricity, and telephone service into the building. (p. 12)

Web—the middle part of an I Beam. (pp. 34 and 45)

OTHER TITLES IN THE POPULAR *LET'S GO* SERIES

Science

to an Atomic Energy Town
to a Planetarium
to a Rocket Base
on a Space Trip
to a Weather Station
to the Moon
to a Fish Hatchery

Health

to a Dentist
to a Hospital

Communications

to a Telephone Company
to a Television Station

Food and Clothing

to a Bakery
to a Clothing Factory
to a Farm

Commerce and Industry

to an Automobile Factory
to a Steel Mill
to a Paper Mill
to a Stock Exchange

Transportation

to a Jetport
to a Harbor
to Build a Suspension Bridge

Conservation

to a National Park
to Stop Air Pollution
to Stop Water Pollution

American History

to an Indian Cliff Dwelling

Armed Services

to West Point
to the U.S. Coast Guard Academy
Aboard an Atomic Submarine

Government—Local

to a City Hall
to Vote

Government—National and International

to the Capitol
to the F.B.I.
to the U.S. Mint
to the White House
to See Congress at Work
to the Peace Corps

Recreation

to a Zoo
to a Football Game

Community—Government

to a Bank
to a Service Station
to a Newspaper
to a Supermarket
to Build a Skyscraper

Community—Commercial

to a Firehouse
to a Library
to a Police Station
to a Post Office
to a Sanitation Department
to a School

Geography

to Europe
to India
to Africa